BRAY IRELAND TRAVEL GUIDE 2023

Uncover the Hidden
Treasures and
Breathtaking Wonders
of this Irish Gem.

ELORA
MACKENZIE

TABLE OF CONTENTS

About Bray

Ireland's County Wicklow is home to the thriving coastal community of Bray. It provides a quick respite from the busy metropolis while offering a variety of sites and activities to enjoy. It is located just south of Dublin. Bray has gained popularity as a tourist attraction among both locals and visitors due to its lovely beachfront, breathtaking scenery, and interesting history.

1.1.1 **Location and Geography**

The Wicklow Mountains and the Irish Sea are located between Bray and provide stunning natural surroundings. The town is located on Ireland's east coast, some 20 kilometres (12 miles) south of Dublin's downtown. Its ideal position provides quick access to both Dublin's cultural and historical gems and County Wicklow's calm beauty.

1.1.2 **Culture and History**

There are several historical sites and landmarks in Bray that serve as reminders of the town's long and varied history. The town was once a modest fishing community that grew into a thriving coastal resort during the Victorian era. The striking Victorian architecture from this era, like the well-known Bray promenade and the scattered Martello Towers around the shoreline, is still evident today.

1.1.3 The Community and Local Culture

The friendly locals and active cultural scene make Bray an inviting and warm community. The community embraces both its historical legacy and contemporary advancements, resulting in a distinctive fusion of traditional charm and modern vigour. Bray offers tourists a chance to fully experience local culture by hosting several festivals and events that highlight local talent, including music, art, and cuisine, throughout the year.

Why Travel to Bray?

Travellers find Bray to be an appealing location because of the wide variety of sights and activities it provides. Here are a few explanations as to why you ought to think about going to Bray:

1.2.1 **Unspoiled Beauty**

Bray's breathtaking natural scenery is one of its key attractions. Sand beaches, the beautiful Bray Head, a towering cliff that offers breathtaking panoramic views of the Irish Sea, and a gorgeous beachfront complete the town's many blessings. Outdoor pursuits like riding, hiking, and water sports are abundant for nature lovers.

1.2.2 The seafront and promenade in Bray

The promenade in Bray, which offers a lovely walk along the sea, is a highlight of the community. Enjoy the lively environment while taking a stroll and breathing in the clean sea air. A vibrant and pleasurable atmosphere is created for tourists of all ages along the seashore thanks to the charming cafes, eateries, and amusement arcades that dot the area.

1.2.3 Historical and cultural landmarks

There are many historical and cultural places to discover in Bray. The Bray Heritage Centre offers an intriguing look into the town's past by showcasing items and tales that show how it has changed over time. A stately country estate with wonderfully planted gardens that provide a calm respite from the rush and bustle of daily life is Kilruddery House and Gardens, which is also open to visitors.

1.2.4 Outdoor Activities

Bray is a paradise for adventure and exploration for outdoor enthusiasts. Take a trek to the top of Bray Head for breathtaking panoramas of the Wicklow Mountains and the surrounding shoreline. The renowned Bray Golf Club, which offers a difficult course set against a backdrop of natural beauty, is where golfers can start their round. Fans of water sports can partake in activities like kayaking, paddle boarding, and swimming in the chilly Irish Sea.

1.2.5 **Dublin's proximity**

Being close to Dublin is one of the many perks of visiting Bray. The town is easily accessible from the capital city, making it a great starting point for day trips to Dublin's cultural and historical attractions. Visitors may easily travel to the bustling city, see well-known sites like Trinity College and Dublin Castle, or enjoy shopping, dining, and entertainment options.

1.2.6 **A welcoming atmosphere for Families**

There are several family-friendly attractions and activities in Bray. Children should visit the National Sea Creatures Centre to wonder about marine creatures and learn about the value of ocean protection. The town also organises the famous Bray Air Display, which attracts guests of all ages and features aerobatic performances and aircraft exhibitions.

1.2.7 A Bustling Restaurant and Entertainment District

A diverse selection of eateries, cafes, bars, and pubs can be found in Bray, which has a thriving dining and entertainment scene. Bray has selections to satisfy every taste, whether you're looking for traditional Irish food, global flavours, or a comfortable pub setting. Experience local artisan brews, take in live music performances, or simply have a delicious meal while taking in the bustling ambiance of the town.

1.2.8 **Gateway to County Wicklow**

Bray serves as a starting point for travellers to discover County Wicklow's famed natural beauty and tourist attractions. You might travel not far to find the stunning Glendalough, a valley with a historic monastery and serene lakes. The Wicklow Mountains National Park provides several chances for biking, hiking, and taking in the pristine beauty of nature.

In conclusion, Bray is a desirable tourism destination because of the alluring combination of its natural beauty, historical charm, and energetic atmosphere. Bray has something to offer everyone, whether you're looking for family-friendly activities, cultural experiences, outdoor excursions, or a convenient base for visiting Dublin and County Wicklow. Plan your trip to this charming coastal town and learn about the special gems that are waiting for you there.

ORGANISING Y OUR TRAVEL

2.1 The Best Time to Go

It's crucial to think about the ideal time to visit Bray based on your tastes and the activities you want to partake in while making travel plans. When choosing the best time for your Bray journey, keep the following variables in mind:

2.1.1 **Climate**

A temperate marine climate characterises Bray, with chilly winters and warm summers. Its seaside location and proximity to the mountains have an impact on the weather. The warmest months are typically June through August when daily highs range from 15°C to 20°C (59°F to 68°F). The best time of year for visiting the beach, engaging in outdoor activities, and discovering the town's attractions. The seasons of spring (March to May) and fall (September to November) are ideal for sightseeing and enjoying nature because they are milder and less congested. Even while winter (December to February) brings colder weather, it can still be a delightful time to go, especially around the holidays when the town is decked up in cheer.

2.1.2 Festivals and Crowds

The busiest times of year in Bray are often the summer months, especially July and August. The town is a well-liked coastal resort, and lots of people come here to take advantage of the beaches, activities, and festivals. If you want a more sedate trip, think about going in the shoulder seasons of spring or autumn when there are fewer visitors and you can take your time seeing the sites. However, it's important to keep in mind that Bray also stages its yearly Bray Air Display during the summer, an exciting air show that draws tourists from all over the world.

2.1.3 **Festivals and Events**

Bray features several events and festivals throughout the year, giving you still more justification for making travel arrangements. You might want to check the neighbourhood event calendar for more fascinating events in addition to the Bray Air Display, which happens in July. This could include sporting events, art shows, music festivals, and cultural festivals. Attending these events might improve your experience and give you a deeper sense of the lively spirit of the area.

2.2 Transportation to Bray

2.2.1 By Air

Flying into Dublin Airport (DUB) is the most practical way to get to Bray if you're coming from abroad. One of the busiest airports in Europe, Dublin Airport is served by a large number of international carriers. You have a few ways to get to Bray from the airport:

- **By Car**: Renting a car at the airport allows you the freedom to independently explore Bray and the nearby areas. The M50 and N11 motorways used to go from the airport to Bray in around 40 minutes.

- **By Public Transportation:** Two bus lines run between Dublin Airport and Bray that are convenient and reasonably priced. These are Aircoach and Airlink Express. While the Airlink Express bus takes you to Dublin City Center where you can change to a train or bus to reach Bray, the Aircoach provides a direct service from the airport to Bray.

2.2.2 By Railroad

Irish Rail's DART (Dublin Area Rapid Transit) service makes it easy to get to Bray and has great rail connections. The DART travels a beautiful seaside route and provides breathtaking vistas. From stations like Connolly, Pearse, or Tara Street, you can board a DART train if you're travelling from Dublin's city centre. Bray is one of the stops along the railway, and the trip takes about 40 minutes.

2.2.3 By Bus

Bray is connected to Dublin and other nearby towns by several bus services. The 145 and 45A buses, which offer direct links to Dublin City Center, are among the frequently run routes the Dublin Bus service operates to and from Bray. Additionally, Bus Éireann has interstate services that stop in Bray, making it simple to travel from other regions of Ireland.

2.3 Bray's Local Transportation

2.3.1 **Strolling**

The small town of Bray is conveniently walkable. A popular location for leisurely strolling, the oceanfront promenade offers stunning views and access to several activities. It is convenient to travel around without any transportation because many of the town's eateries, shops, and amenities are close to one another.

2.3.2 **Biking**

In Bray, cycling is a common form of transportation, and the community has created an infrastructure that is bike-friendly and designated bicycle routes. Bicycles are available for rent at several nearby businesses if you'd rather explore the neighbourhood on two wheels. Cycling enables you to travel further and explore more of the surrounding area, which includes the picturesque Wicklow Mountains.

2.3.3 Public Transportation

Public transportation is readily available in Bray, making it simple to get around town and to nearby locations. The previously mentioned DART train service is a practical means of getting around the coastal regions, including visiting nearby towns like Greystones. Local bus services that connect Bray with other areas of Wicklow and Dublin include the Dublin Bus routes and Bus Éireann services, adding to the area's transportation options.

2.3.4 **Ride-Sharing and Taxis**

In Bray, taxis are easily accessible, and you can find taxi ranks all over the city, including along the seafront and in the town centre. Taxis are a practical and comfortable means of transportation for getting around town or for longer distances. In Bray, there are also ride-sharing services like Uber that serve as an alternative to standard taxis.

2.3.5 **Auto Lease**

There are car rental services available in Bray and at Dublin Airport if you prefer the independence and convenience of having your transportation. By renting a car, you can travel more independently throughout the area and visit destinations that might be more remote or difficult to reach by public transportation. It's important to keep in mind, though, that parking and traffic can be difficult during busy times, particularly in the summer.

Finally, when organising your trip to Bray, think about the best time to go based on the weather, crowds, and events. The primary entry point for international travellers is Dublin Airport, from which Bray can be reached via several different modes of transportation, including trains, buses, and car rentals. Walking and cycling are the best modes of transportation once in Bray, while public transportation, taxis, and ride-sharing services offer practical options for getting around and exploring the surrounding area. Making the most of everything the town of Bray and its surroundings have to offer can be assured with careful planning, resulting in a hassle-free and enjoyable trip.

TOP BRAY ATTRACTIONS

3.1 Bray Seafront and Promenade

One of the most well-liked tourist destinations in the city is the bustling Bray Promenade and Seafront. The promenade, which stretches the length of the shoreline, offers delightful walking opportunities as well as breathtaking views of the Irish Sea. Enjoy the cool sea breeze while taking a stroll along the promenade and taking in the energetic atmosphere. You can stop for a bite to eat or indulge in a sweet treat at any of the charming cafés, restaurants, and ice cream stands you come across along the road. Visitors of all ages can have fun on the seafront's amusement arcades, mini-golf courses, and fairground rides.

3.2 Bray Head

Bray Head is a famous landmark and a must-see destination for outdoor enthusiasts, proudly dominating the town. The cliff provides expansive views of the Irish Sea, the coast of Bray, and the surroundings. Follow the Bray Head Cliff

Walk, a lovely path that meanders up the hillside, to get to the summit. The moderately challenging walk takes about two hours to complete. Once at the summit, you'll be rewarded with beautiful sights that make the effort worthwhile. Don't forget to bring your camera to capture the lovely scenery.

3.3 Bray Heritage Centre

Immerse yourself in the rich history of Bray by visiting the Bray Heritage Centre. Located in a historic structure on the beachfront, the centre provides a fascinating peek into the town's past. Explore interactive exhibits, antiques, and displays that chronicle the growth of Bray from its fishing town origins to a Victorian-era coastal resort. Learn about the town's notable residents, significant events, and cultural legacy through interesting multimedia presentations. The Bray Heritage Centre offers a comprehensive grasp of the town's history and is a fantastic starting point for knowing more about Bray's unique character.

3.4   Kilruddery House and Gardens

Located just outside Bray, Kilruddery House and Gardens is a spectacular country estate that shows the stunning architecture and well-planted gardens. This historic house has been the ancestral home of the Brabazon family since the 17th century and is open to the public for guided tours. Explore the sumptuous interiors, decorated with historical furniture, artwork, and delicate detailing. Afterward, meander through the large grounds, boasting manicured lawns, vivid flower beds, and quiet lakes. Kilruddery House and Gardens give a calm getaway from the rush and bustle of Bray and offer an insight into the grandeur of Ireland's past.

3.5 Powerscourt Estate and Gardens

A short drive from Bray, Powerscourt Estate and Gardens is a lovely site that exhibits the natural beauty of Ireland. The estate is home to one of the most impressive gardens in the country, boasting traditional terraces, attractive lakes, and a rich array of plants and flowers. Explore the Japanese gardens, wander along tree-lined pathways, and marvel at the carefully groomed lawns. Another magnificent Palladian mansion that merits a visit is Powerscourt House. Several shops, boutiques, and a renowned café are housed inside for your convenience. You may connect with nature and take in the natural beauty of the Irish countryside at the Powerscourt Estate and Gardens, which offers a tranquil and picturesque refuge.

3.6 National Sea Life Center

A trip to the National Sea Life Centre is

essential for ocean lovers. This interactive aquarium offers a chance to explore the amazing underwater world and is situated on the waterfront. Discover a variety of exhibitions showcasing various marine environments, including the Irish Sea and tropical oceans. Get up close and personal with a variety of marine life, such as sharks, rays, seahorses, and vibrant tropical fish. Learn about the need to protect our seas and marine conservation activities. Visitors of all ages can have an instructive and exciting experience at the National Sea Life Centre.

3.7 Farmers' Market in Killruddery

Don't miss the Killruddery Farmers' Market if you're in Bray on a Saturday. This vibrant market, which is held inside the storied Killruddery House and Gardens, has the finest in regional foods, crafts, and vegetables. Wander among the booths selling organic meats, cheeses, fresh fruits and veggies, homemade baked goods, and more. Examine delectable foods, converse with regional producers, and take in the lively ambiance. The Killruddery Farmers' Market is a wonderful place to sample local cuisine and support small businesses.

In conclusion, many attractions in Bray cater

to a range of tastes and interests. There is something for everyone to enjoy, from the picturesque beachfront promenade to the imposing Bray Head and the rich history displayed at the Bray Heritage Centre. Offering tranquil escapes in stunning natural surroundings are the adjacent Powerscourt Estate and Kilruddery House and Gardens. The National Sea Life Centre offers an immersive experience for marine aficionados. Additionally, the Killruddery Farmers' Market provides a pleasant culinary experience for visitors who want to discover regional delicacies. Plan your trip to Bray and learn about the great sights that make this seaside community a very unforgettable vacation spot.

BRAY OUTDOOR ACTIVITIES

4.1 Nature hikes and walks

Because Bray is surrounded by such stunning scenery, it is a great place for outdoor enthusiasts and wildlife lovers. Here are a few of the best places to go hiking and doing nature walks in and near Bray:

- The Bray Head Cliff Walk is a well-liked path that provides breathtaking views over the Irish Sea and the surroundings. The trail ascends Bray Head, a notable hill with a panoramic view of the town, from the beachfront promenade. The trail offers panoramic views, rocky cliffs, and a variety of flora and animals as you stroll along it. The moderately challenging trek takes about two hours to complete. For those looking for breathtaking views and a sense of adventure, it's a must-do activity.

- Consider the Bray to Greystones Cliff Walk if you're looking for a longer, more difficult hike. Between Bray and the nearby town of Greystones, this beautiful trail follows the ocean.

Along the walk, you may see the Irish Sea and its rocky cliffs on one side and its lush flora on the other, providing stunning vistas. The hike is approximately 7 kilometres (4.3 miles) long and takes three hours to finish. It's a great chance to take in the area's coastline scenery and get some energising workouts.

- **Killruddery House and Gardens:** Although not a designated hiking trail, the Killruddery House and Gardens' grounds provide many chances for strolls through magnificent scenery. Wander through the vast gardens and down the tree-lined walks to find quiet retreats. The estate offers a tranquil retreat from the bustle of daily life with its lovely vistas, well-kept lawns, and tranquil lakes.

- A short distance from Bray, the Wicklow Mountains National Park provides a plethora of chances for outdoor recreation and adventure. The park's expansive region is home to breathtaking mountains, glacial valleys, and crystal-clear lakes.

There are many
trails available for
hikers to select
from, each catered
to a distinct ability
level and
inclination. The
Wicklow
Mountains
National Park
offers a variety of
activities, whether
you're searching
for a strenuous
walk to a
mountaintop or a
stroll through
tranquil
woodlands.

4.2 Bray Golf Club

Bray Golf Club is a top
destination for golf fans.
This picturesque golf
course, which is located
outside of the city,
provides golfers of all
skill levels with a
difficult and pleasurable
experience. The 18-hole
parkland course with

sweeping views of the surroundings, well-kept greens, and undulating fairways. Golfers can try their abilities while taking in the area's stunning natural surroundings. A driving range and putting greens are available for practice at the club, and there is also a clubhouse where you can unwind and enjoy refreshments after a game.

4.3 Water Activities on Bray Beach

Bray is a great place for fans of water sports due to its proximity to the Irish Sea. For those wishing to make a splash, Bray Beach offers a variety of activities. Here are some water sports you may participate in:

- **Swimming:** Enjoy a cool swim in

Bray Beach's crystal-clear waters. During the summer, there are dedicated swimming areas on the beach where you may take a leisurely dip or participate in watersports while a lifeguard keeps an eye on you. Families and beginners with little swimming experience can enjoy the shallow waters close to the coast.

- **Surfing:** Bray Beach is renowned for its surfers' paradise, especially in the fall and winter when the waves are at their peak. You can rent equipment or enrol in surf classes given by nearby surf schools if you are an experienced surfer or want to learn the sport. For surfers, catching a wave and riding it along the coast is an amazing experience.

- **Stand-Up Paddleboarding (SUP):** This water sport has grown in popularity recently, and Bray Beach is a great location for it. Navigate the calm waters while standing on a paddleboard to get a distinctive view of the shoreline. Regardless of your level of competence, SUP offers a fun and interesting way to explore the sea.

- **Kayaking:** Use a kayak to explore the shoreline and travel into undiscovered coves and caves. Rent a kayak and paddle along the shore while admiring the breathtaking scenery and the serenity of the ocean. There are also guided kayaking tours that give you the chance to have an exhilarating adventure while learning about the local marine ecology and history.

Jet skiing is an exciting option if you're looking for an adrenaline rush. Experience the thrill of speeding across the waves on a powerful jet ski while feeling the wind in your hair and the spray of the ocean. You may have an amazing water adventure by renting a jet ski at Bray Beach.

In conclusion, Bray provides a wide range of outdoor activities to accommodate different interests and physical abilities. You may immerse yourself in the breathtaking coastal and alpine surroundings that surround the town by hiking and taking nature hikes. In addition to swimming, surfing, stand-up paddleboarding, kayaking, and jet skiing on Bray Beach, golf fans can tee off at Bray Golf Club. Everyone looking to connect with nature and enjoy the great outdoors will find something in Bray, whether they choose a stroll, an adrenaline-pumping adventure, or a tranquil round of golf.

EXPERIENCES WITH CULTURE AND HISTORY IN BRAY

St. Peter's Cathedral

Bray's St. Peter's Church is a well-known monument with major historical and cultural significance. This lovely church, which lies in the centre of town, was built in the early 19th century. Gothic and Romanesque elements are used to create the architecture, which also includes a spectacular bell tower, gorgeous stained glass windows, and complex brickwork.

Enter to see the magnificent decor and take in the serene ambiance. St. Peter's Church serves as a location for concerts and other cultural events in addition to being a place of worship, which increases its cultural relevance in the neighbourhood.

5.2 The Victorian Era in Bray

The architectural and historical sites of Bray still reflect the town's rich Victorian past. Bray changed from a tiny fishing community to a chic coastal resort during the 19th century, drawing tourists looking for entertainment and relaxation. The opulent structures and magnificent promenades along the coast are clear examples of Victorian influence. Admire the well-preserved Victorian architecture, which includes elaborate hotels, magnificent terraces, and attractive cottages, as you wander quietly along the promenade. The town's cultural appeal is enhanced by the Victorian legacy, which attests to Bray's historical importance.

Martello Towers

The early 19th-century defence constructions known as Martello Towers, which were constructed along the Irish coast, are another element of Bray's cultural and historical landscape. One of these towers, the Bray Head Martello Tower, is perched atop Bray Head and provides sweeping views over the area.

These towers were built as a line of defence against prospective invasions by Napoleon, and they had a big impact on Irish military history. Although several towers are no longer open to the public, Bray Head Martello Tower offers a chance to tour the inside and discover their historical significance. This intriguing event sheds light on Ireland's historical development and the strategic significance of these defences.

5.4 Events & Festivals

Every year, Bray holds several festivals and events that highlight the town's diverse culture and give locals and tourists alike a chance to gather together and celebrate. These major celebrations and events took place in Bray:

- The annual Bray Jazz Festival, which takes place in May, attracts jazz fans from near and far. Jazz performers from around the world and the local community play during the festival in a variety of locations around the city. The Bray Jazz Festival offers a vibrant atmosphere and a chance to fully immerse oneself in the jazz world, with events ranging from raucous concerts to intimate performances.
- Bray Summerfest is a major event on the town's

schedule of events that takes place throughout the summer. This fun-filled event for families features a variety of entertainment options, such as funfair rides, live music, street performances, and fireworks displays. It's a wonderful chance to take in the colourful environment, experience regional cuisine and handicrafts, and take part in fun activities suitable for people of all ages.

- **Bray Air Display:** Held every year in July, the Bray Air Display is one of the biggest free-air displays in

Europe.
Thousands of people congregate along the beachfront for this exciting event to witness breathtaking aerobatic displays by both military and civilian aircraft. The air show also includes family-friendly entertainment, food vendors, and ground exhibits. This weekend is the pinnacle of Bray's summer calendar and is filled with high-flying excitement.

- **Bray literary festival:** The Bray Literary Festival, which features authors from both domestic and foreign countries, is a treat for readers. The festival offers a forum for literary discussion and celebration of the written word through author readings, panel discussions, workshops, and book signings. The Bray Literary Festival provides an inspiring and interesting experience, regardless of whether you are a voracious reader or an aspiring writer.

These festivals and events showcase Bray's thriving cultural scene and offer chances to interact with the locals, celebrate music and the arts, and take in the bustling atmosphere of the town.

In conclusion, Bray provides a variety of historical and cultural activities that let tourists explore the town's past and become a part of its thriving cultural scene. There are many opportunities to learn about Bray's history, from the historical importance of St. Peter's Church to the Victorian architecture that adorns the town's beachfront. The Martello Towers serve as a reminder of Ireland's military past, and the festivals and events that take place all year round highlight the vibrant and hospitable nature of the neighbourhood. Bray has something to offer every history and culture fan, whether they are interested in historical sites, cultural activities, or simply absorbing the local ambiance.

FOOD AND DINING IN BRAY

6.1 Best Restaurants and Pubs

The culinary scene in Bray is diversified, with a selection of dining establishments to suit every preference and price range. The following are some of the town's top eateries and bars:

- Platform Pizza is a well-known restaurant serving delectable wood-fired pizzas and is situated on the seaside in Bray. They make delectable concoctions that satisfy all tastes, including vegetarian and vegan options, using fresh, locally sourced ingredients. It's a great option for a casual eating experience, with a relaxed ambiance and helpful service.

- Box Burger is the place to go if you're in the mood for a delicious burger. This hip restaurant, which is located in the centre of Bray, offers gourmet burgers with distinctive flavour combinations. For burger lovers, Box Burger offers a spectacular eating experience with everything from traditional beef burgers to innovative versions made with locally sourced ingredients.

- **The Harbour Bar:** If you want to enjoy a real Irish pub, you must go there. The Harbour Bar is popular with locals and tourists alike for its warm and inviting ambiance, live music events, and an extensive assortment of drinks, including Irish whiskey and craft brews. Grab a pint, take in the real pub atmosphere, and maybe even listen to some traditional Irish music.

- **Campo de Fiori:** Campo de' Fiori is a great option if you're in the mood for Italian food. The menu of this family-run eatery is influenced by the tastes of Italy and features dishes like homemade pasta, wood-fired pizza, and decadent desserts. Campo de' Fiori offers a real flavour of Italy in the centre of Bray thanks to its pleasant interior and excellent service.
- The Boxty House serves up traditional Irish food with a contemporary touch. Boxty, a classic Irish potato pancake that is

offered with a variety of fillings and sides, is the specialty of this quaint restaurant. The Boxty House offers a distinctive dining experience that honours Irish traditions, with everything from hearty stews to delectable seafood dishes.

6.2 Customary Irish Food

Bray offers a variety of traditional Irish restaurants that highlight the greatest regional cuisines. The following foods, which range from hearty stews to recently caught seafood, are worth trying:

- **Irish Stew:** Made with delicate lamb, root

vegetables, and flavorful herbs, Irish stew is a traditional Irish dish that is hearty and comforting. The flavorful stew is made slowly and is excellent for keeping you warm on a cool day.

- **Boxty:** A traditional Irish potato pancake, as was previously noted. With different ingredients including beef, poultry, or veggies, it can be eaten as a side dish or as a main entrée. Boxty is a flexible and mouthwatering choice that honours Ireland's culinary heritage.
- Being a coastal community, Bray

is well-known for its fresh seafood. To enjoy the taste of the sea, try a bowl of creamy seafood chowder. This substantial soup is a favourite among both locals and tourists and is packed with a variety of fish, shrimp, mussels, and other shellfish.

- A slice of soda bread is a must-have for any Irish supper. The basic components of this classic Irish bread are flour, buttermilk, baking soda, and salt. The end product is a hearty, dense bread with a hint of sweetness that goes great with soups, stews, or simply some Irish butter.

6.3 Regional Specialties

Additionally, Bray offers certain regional cuisine delicacies that are intriguing to try:

- Bray is renowned for its premium smoked salmon, which is sourced from local coastal waters. To improve the flavour and texture of this delicacy, it is meticulously cured and smoked. Take it alone, with some brown bread and lemon juice, or as part of a mouthwatering seafood platter.
- **Wicklow Lamb:** The

county of Wicklow, where Bray is situated, is well known for its flavorful lamb. Wicklow lamb produces a soft and tasty meat that complements the area's natural beauty and is raised on the region's lush green pastures. To enjoy this regional specialty, look for lamb dishes on the menus of nearby eateries.

- **Wicklow Cheeses:** The fertile farms and undulating hills of Wicklow make it the perfect place to make cheese. Try some artisanal cheeses from nearby producers like Wicklow Blue and Wicklow Bán to see the skill and commitment to quality that goes into making these delicious dairy treats.

To sum up, Bray has a varied culinary scene with a selection of dining options to suit every taste. There is something for every food enthusiast, from gourmet burgers and wood-fired pizzas to traditional Irish meals and regional delicacies. If you're searching for a quaint pub, a family-run eatery, or a taste of authentic Irish cuisine, Bray boasts a variety of restaurants that are sure to satisfy your appetite and leave you wanting more.

SHOPPING IN BRAY

7.1 Memorabilia and Gifts

For presents and mementos to remember your visit, Bray provides a wide range of possibilities. Here are some suggestions for finding special souvenirs:

- **Bray Tourist Office:** If you're looking to buy souvenirs, the Bray Tourist Office is an excellent place to start. They provide a variety of regionally inspired products, such as postcards, keychains, magnets, and clothes with the town's emblem or famous sites. It's a practical one-stop shop for obtaining mementos of your time in Bray.

- Explore the quaint artisan and gift shops that are sprinkled around Bray. These shops offer a variety of handcrafted and one-of-a-kind items while showcasing the work of regional craftsmen. Look for items such as ceramics, jewellery, paintings, and other crafts that showcase the community's talent and ingenuity. These stores are fantastic places to find one-of-a-kind presents to bring home or to treat yourself to something special.

- **Bookstores:** If you enjoy reading, peruse the Bray area's bookstores to uncover a unique piece of literature. Learn about Irish authors, travel guides to Bray and its surroundings, or books with local settings.
Bookstores are the ideal place to find special and long-lasting souvenirs because they frequently contain a well-chosen collection of books that represent the essence of the local culture.

7.2 Local Stores and Markets

Bray has several neighbourhood markets and stores where you can browse a variety of goods in addition to souvenir purchasing. Here are some locations to explore:

- **Bray Farmers' Market:** The lively Bray Farmers' Market is held every Saturday and features a wide selection of fresh fruit, baked goods, artisanal goods, and crafts. It's a wonderful chance to support regional farmers and producers while indulging in delectable snacks and finding interesting handmade goods.

- **Bray Main Street:** Take a stroll down this lively road and browse the stores and boutiques that line it. A variety of regional and independent shops may be found here, selling everything from clothing and accessories to home goods and specialised cuisine. Spend some time exploring the shops, chatting with the welcoming store owners, and finding hidden treasures.
- **Quinsboro Road Market:** This market, which is

situated on Quinsboro Road, sells a variety of products, including clothing, accessories, home goods, and more. It's a bustling market where you may look around the stalls, talk to the sellers, and discover intriguing things that capture your eye.

- Although it is officially outside of Bray but close by, the Killruddery Farmers' Market is worth a trip. This market, which is held on Saturdays, features artisanal cuisine, local crafts, and more. It's a wonderful chance to get to know the locals, enjoy some delectable cuisine, and buy some specialty items made in the area.

- You can find local goods, interact with vendors, and support the neighbourhood by buying at these neighbourhood markets and stores in Bray. These locations offer a glimpse into the thriving local environment and possibilities to take a piece of Bray home with you, whether you're looking for fresh vegetables, handmade products, or one-of-a-kind items.

In conclusion, there are many alternatives for selecting gifts and souvenirs to take home as a reminder of your trip when shopping in Bray. There are numerous options to find one-of-a-kind and sentimental objects, whether you prefer to peruse craft and gift shops, visit local markets and shops, or explore the tourist office. The shopping environment in Bray represents the spirit of the community and offers an opportunity to support small companies and craftsmen by purchasing locally made goods, fresh fruit, and souvenirs with regional themes.

BRAY'S NIGHTLIFE AND

8.1 Bars and Pubs

With several pubs and bars to suit all preferences, Bray has a thriving nightlife. Here are some well-known places to check out:

- The Porterhouse Bray is a well-known bar and microbrewery that serves a variety of craft brews, including their creations. It's a terrific spot to unwind and enjoy a pint with friends because of the welcoming atmosphere and live music on some nights.
- The Harbour Bar is a popular tavern as well as a

popular cultural destination, as was already mentioned. It draws both locals and tourists due to its traditional charm, live music events, and broad drink menu. With a few drinks in hand, kick back, unwind, and take in the warm and welcoming atmosphere.

- **The Martello Hotel:** The Martello Hotel has a bustling bar where live music is frequently played. Both locals and visitors frequent this well-liked location to unwind with a drink while tapping their feet to the sounds of excellent performers. In addition, the pub has a welcoming environment and a variety of pub food.

- The Hibernia is a chic pub with a broad selection of drinks, including craft beers, cocktails, and a finely chosen list of wines, that is situated on Bray's coastline. It's a terrific location for hanging out with friends, unwinding, and taking in the sea views while sipping your favourite beverage.

8.2 Live music venues

There are several places to see live music

performances in Bray, which is noted for having a thriving music culture. Here are a few places to note:

- **The Harbour Bar:** The Harbour Bar deserves to be mentioned once more in the live music section. It frequently presents live music performances by both local and visiting musicians from a range of genres, such as folk, rock, traditional Irish music, and more. An unforgettable musical experience is created by the cosy environment and energised audience.
- **The Martello Hotel:** In

addition to its popular bar, the hotel frequently presents live music performances by regional bands and artists. In a laid-back and welcoming atmosphere, enjoy an evening of live music by checking their calendar before your visit.

- **The Mermaid Arts Centre:** The Mermaid Arts Centre is primarily a performing arts centre, although it also offers live music events and shows by regional and worldwide performers on occasion. To find out if any musical performances coincide with your visit, check out their event schedule.

- **Bray Jazz Festival:** As was previously noted, the Bray Jazz Festival is held in May and draws jazz fans from near and far. During the festival, a wide range of jazz performers play at several locations throughout the city. It's a wonderful chance to become fully immersed in the jazz genre and take in outstanding live performances.
- These Bray pubs, bars, and live music venues offer a vibrant and enjoyable nightlife. There are many options

available, whether you want to relax with a drink with friends, take in live music, or become involved in the local music scene. Everybody can enjoy and make lifelong memories in Bray's nightlife, which features everything from jazz and rock to traditional Irish music.

In conclusion, Bray's entertainment options and nightlife cater to a wide range of interests and likes. Bray boasts a variety of businesses to suit your preferences, whether you're looking for a tranquil drink at a classic pub, an exciting night of live music, or a combination of the two. Don't miss the chance to catch live music

performances at places
like The Harbour Bar,
The Martello Hotel, and
The Mermaid Arts
Centre as you explore
the neighbourhood's
pubs and bars. Make the
most of your nights in
Bray by taking in the
lively ambiance and the
vibrant local music
scene.

DAY TRIPS
FROM BRAY

9.1 Dublin City

Dublin, the country's
capital, is a must-see
location with a wide
variety of attractions,
history, and culture. You
may simply take a day
trip from Bray to
experience Dublin's top
attractions. Consider
these major attractions:

- Visit Ireland's
  oldest university,

Trinity College, and take in the breathtaking campus while learning about the Book of Kells. Don't pass up the chance to view the magnificent Book of Kells, an illuminated manuscript from the ninth century.

- **Guinness Storehouse:** At the Guinness Storehouse, learn about the origins and brewing techniques of Ireland's most renowned brew. Visit the Gravity Bar for a tour, discover how to pour the ideal pint, and take in the expansive views of Dublin.
- **Dublin Castle:** Take a

tour of this historic building, which was the centre of British rule in Ireland for many years. Visit the Chapel Royal, the State Apartments, and the breathtaking grounds.

- **Temple Bar:** Get lost in the lively ambiance of Dublin's cultural district, Temple Bar. There are several bars, eateries, art galleries, and outdoor concerts in this bustling neighbourhood.
- **St. Patrick's Cathedral:** Take in the splendour of Ireland's biggest cathedral as you awe at its size. Explore its fascinating history

and spectacular architecture, which dates back to the 12th century.

9.2 Glendalough

Glendalough, a lovely valley recognized for its natural beauty and historical significance, is situated in the centre of the Wicklow Mountains. Both lovers of the outdoors and those who enjoy history should visit here. Highlights consist of:

- Visit the historic monastery at Glendalough, which St. Kevin founded in the sixth century. Admire the round tower, recognizable stone crosses, and several churches and other structures that are in ruins.

- **Glendalough National Park:** Explore the breathtaking Glendalough National Park on a leisurely walk or hike. Take time to relax and take in the beauty of the mountains, lakes, and forests.
- **Upper Lake and Lower Lake:** Glendalough is made up of two glacial lakes, Upper Lake and Lower Lake. Enjoy the surrounding scenery while taking a stroll around the lakes and taking in the crisp mountain air.
- Glendalough has a variety of hiking trails to suit hikers

of all fitness levels and interests. Enter nature by setting out on a rewarding hike to discover the mountains, valleys, and waterfalls.

9.3 Wicklow Mountains

The Wicklow Mountains, also known as the "Garden of Ireland," provide a breathtaking setting for adventure and outdoor pursuits. What you can enjoy, from picturesque roads to hiking trails:

- **Sally Gap:** Take a scenic drive via the mountain pass of Sally Gap, which provides mesmerising views of the surroundings. You pass through valleys, rolling hills, and moorlands covered with heather on the winding route.

- **Lough Tay:** Due to its peat-coloured waters and white sand beach, Lough Tay is known as the "Guinness Lake" and is a beautiful location to visit. Relax in this peaceful environment while admiring the beauty of the lake and the mountains nearby.
- **Wicklow Way:** Lace up your hiking boots and set off on a portion of Ireland's first long-distance hiking trail with waymarks, the

Wicklow Way. As you hike this well-known track, take in the breathtaking views, serene woodlands, and untamed mountain scenery.

- Visit the majestic Powerscourt Estate, which is situated at the base of the Wicklow Mountains. View the expansive vistas of the estate, the beautiful formal gardens, and Powerscourt House's architecture.

These day trip choices from Bray provide you the chance to see some of the most stunning and important landmarks in the region. Whether you decide to travel to Dublin City, take in the scenic splendour of Glendalough, or explore the Wicklow Mountains, each location offers a distinctive experience and a chance to learn more about Ireland's charm and diversity.

PRACTICAL INFORMATION

10.1 Money and Financial Issues

- Ireland uses the euro (€) as its official currency. For modest transactions and in case you run across businesses that do not take card payments, it is advised to keep some cash on hand.

- **ATMs:** In Bray, there are many ATMs (Automated Teller Machines) where you can withdraw money in the local currency. For information on any fees or withdrawal restrictions for foreign transactions, check with your bank.
- **Credit Cards:** The majority of hotels, restaurants, and retail establishments accept major credit cards including Visa and Mastercard. But it's always a good idea to have some cash on hand as well, particularly

for smaller businesses.

10.2 Emergency Phone Numbers

- **Emergency Services:** Dial 999 or 112 in case of an emergency. You can call these numbers to be connected to the relevant emergency service, such as the police, fire department, or medical aid.
- **Medical Services:** If you need medical attention, there are several hospitals and clinics in and near Bray. Bray Primary Care Centre, Bray Medical Centre, and St.

Columcille's Hospital are a few significant possibilities.

- Check the contact information and location of your country's embassy or consulate before your journey if you need assistance from them. The consulates and embassies of numerous nations can be found in Dublin.

10.3 Communication and Language

- **Language:** English is the main language used in Bray and all of Ireland. Communication with the people won't be a problem because English is commonly spoken and understood.

- **Irish Language:** The Irish language, usually referred to as Gaelic or Irish, is recognized as one of Ireland's official languages. Irish may be used for signs or some phrases, even though it is not typically spoken in daily life in most places, especially in more rural or Gaeltacht (Irish-speaking) communities.

10.4 Regional Customs and Protocol

- **Greetings:** The most typical way to introduce

yourself when meeting someone new in Bray is with a firm handshake. A simple "hello" or "hi" is likewise appropriate in more casual contexts.

- **Tipping:** Tipping is expected in Ireland, particularly in cafes, bars, and restaurants. Depending on the quality of the service, a gratuity of between 10% and 15% of the entire cost is common. Check the bill first, though, as some businesses could add a service fee.
- Being on time is typically required while attending meetings and

appointments in Ireland. It is considered courteous to arrive a few minutes early and to show respect for other people's time.

- **Respect for Culture:** It's crucial to show respect for regional traditions and customs when visiting Bray. Be sensitive to cultural differences, especially while visiting places of worship or taking part in regional festivities.
- Smoking restrictions apply to all enclosed public areas, including bars, restaurants, and public transit. Outside these

places, designated smoking areas are frequently offered. Understanding the regional customs and etiquette of the place you are going is always a good idea. During your visit to Bray, you'll have a more enjoyable and peaceful time if you respect the local way of life.

TIPS FOR TRAVELLERS' SAFETY'S

It can be exciting to visit a new place like Bray, but you should put your safety first while you're there. Observe the following safety advice:

- **Research and Planning:** Before your travel, learn about the regional traditions, legal framework, and any threats. Learn the local emergency phone numbers as well as the address of the closest embassy or consulate.

- **Protect Your Property:** Always keep your personal property secure. Passports, cash, and devices should all be kept in a safe place and a bag or backpack. Be aware of your surroundings and refrain from showing off your affluence.
- Make sure you have a method of staying connected while travelling. Keep your cell device charged, and for emergency communication, have a local SIM

card or Wi-Fi
connection.

- Purchase travel
insurance that
includes coverage
for unexpected
medical expenses,
trip cancellation
or interruption,
and theft or loss of
personal property.
Keep a copy of the
insurance
information on
 and go over the
policy to
understand what
is covered.
- Keep Up With
Local News and
Events, Including
Any Potential
Safety Concerns:
Stay informed. If
your embassy or
consulate is open,
register there so
they can contact
you in an
emergency.

- Use trustworthy, licensed transportation services for your safety. Learn the local traffic regulations if you're renting a car, and practise defensive driving. Be mindful of your surroundings and keep a watch on your valuables when utilising public transportation.
- Use caution when speaking to strangers and exercise good judgement. Be cautious while disclosing personal information and stay away from unpleasant or risky circumstances.

- **Respect Local Laws and Customs:** When visiting a new place, it's important to respect the regional laws, traditions, and cultural standards. When visiting religious sites, especially, dress appropriately, and abide by any local laws or limitations.
- In crowded places like markets, tourist attractions, or on public transportation, be on the lookout for your possessions. Keep your bag or money secure and be on the lookout for pickpockets.
- **Trust Your Gut Feelings:** Trust your gut feelings

and pay attention to them. Get out of a situation if it makes you feel unsafe or uneasy, and ask for help if you need it. Remember that no place to visit is completely risk-free, but you can increase your safety and have a memorable and pleasurable vacation to Bray by being informed, exercising common sense, and taking the appropriate precautions.

CONCLUSION

Bray, Ireland offers a wonderful fusion of the outdoors, history, and welcoming people. By the time we've finished this travel guide to Bray in 2023, it should be clear that this quaint seaside town has plenty to offer everyone.

Outdoor enthusiasts will find lots of possibilities for hiking, nature walks, golfing, and water sports, from the picturesque promenade and seashore to the spectacular Bray Head. Bray's rich background is revealed via its cultural and historical attractions, such as St. Peter's Church, the Victorian era, Martello Towers, and lively festivals and events.

The variety of eating options, which includes everything from traditional Irish meals to regional specialties, will thrill food aficionados. Shopaholics can browse the neighbourhood markets and stores, while those looking for a fun night out can check out the hopping pubs, clubs, and live music venues.

Bray is also a great starting point for day visits to local sights. The Wicklow Mountains, with their picturesque vistas, Glendalough, with its spectacular monastery ruins and natural beauty, and Dublin City, with its historical landmarks and cultural attractions, all provide wonderful experiences nearby.

As with any travel destination, it's crucial to put safety first, respect local traditions, and make appropriate plans. Keep yourself informed, keep your possessions safe, and pay attention to your surroundings.

Bray has something to offer whether you're a fan of the outdoors, interested in history, looking for an exciting new experience, or just want to unwind. It offers the potential to be a memorable location due to its beautiful coastline, energetic environment, and hospitable inhabitants.

Pack your luggage, travel to Bray, and acquaint yourself with the mesmerising culture and natural beauty that this Irish treasure has to offer. Take in the scenery and make lifelong memories as you go. Sláinte!

Printed in Great Britain
by Amazon

25141024R00059